Black-Tailed Prairie Dogs

Written by Jo Windsor

Contents

What are black-tailed prairie dogs?	2
Social animals	4
Groups called coteries	6
A town map	8
Look-outs	10
A cross-section of a prairie dog town	12
Using plants and grasses	14
Prairie dog meetings	16
Kissing!	18
Fighting	20
Grooming	22
Barking and calling	24
It's OK now	26
A day in the life of a black-tailed prairie dog	28
Quiz	30
Glossary	31
Index	32

What are black-tailed prairie dogs?

Black-tailed prairie dogs are light brown, with a round belly, small ears and large black eyes. The tips of their tails are black.

These tubby **rodents** weigh around 1-2 kilos and are about 35-40 centimetres long. Their feet have long sharp claws which they use to dig their **burrows**.

Prairie dogs are related to squirrels, but they are called 'dogs' because they have a high-pitched bark. They are **herbivores**, but eat insects, too.

They have one **litter** of pups a year. There are normally 3-5 pups in a litter.

large black eyes

small ears

long sharp claws

light brown fur

round belly

black tip on tail

A black-tailed prairie dog

Social animals

Black-tailed prairie dogs are **social** animals. They live in huge underground 'towns' on vast areas of land called plains, in North America.

The towns consist of burrows, which have tunnels, entrances and exits. Rooms called **chambers** lead off from the tunnels. Each room is used for a different purpose – sleeping, eating, nursery, bathroom – and has bedding of dry leaves and grass.

As many as 1000 dogs live in large groups in each town.

Black-tailed prairie dogs at one of the entrances to their town on the plains in North America

Groups called coteries

The large groups are divided into smaller groups, called coteries. A coterie consists of dogs that live and work **co-operatively**, and the number of dogs in each coterie is different.

Some coteries have an adult male and three females, and about six pups. Others can be larger, with about 30 dogs altogether.

A coterie of black-tailed prairie dogs

A town map

- The dogs in each coterie in a town live closely together in their burrow.

- They share the tunnels and nesting chambers in their burrow.

- They also share all the jobs that need to be done, such as cleaning out old bedding and acting as look-outs at the entrances.

A burrow in a town seen from below

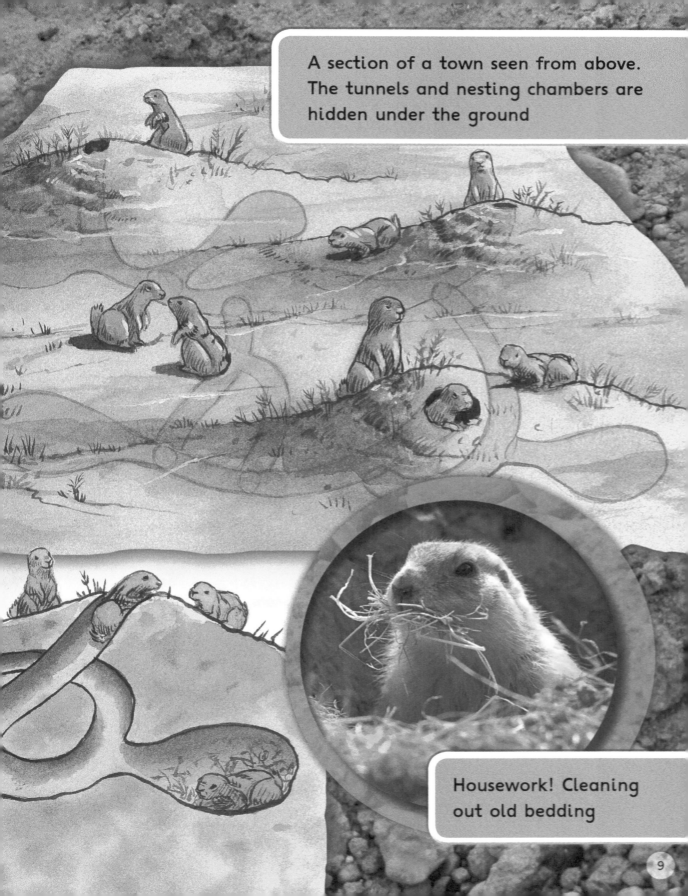

A section of a town seen from above. The tunnels and nesting chambers are hidden under the ground

Housework! Cleaning out old bedding

Look-outs

Prairie dogs build a **mound** of earth at each entrance to a burrow. They dig the earth with their long sharp claws, and push it to the entrance. Then they pack it down with their nose or head until it is hard. This is called tamping. The mounds are about 30 centimetres high.

An entrance to a burrow

Pushing some earth
to an entrance

The dogs build the mounds
for two reasons. When it rains
heavily, the mounds help to
stop the rain from filling up
the tunnels and chambers.
The mounds are also used as
look-outs. The dogs take it
in turns to sit on them and
look out for predators such as
eagles, hawks, snakes, **bobcats**
and **coyotes**.

My turn to be look-out!

A cross-section of a prairie dog town

- The mound at each entrance and exit of a town **prevents** rain water from filling up the tunnels and nesting chambers in the burrows.

- All the tunnels and chambers in a burrow are shared by the members of a coterie in a town.

- The prairie dogs dig about one metre below the ground to make their towns.

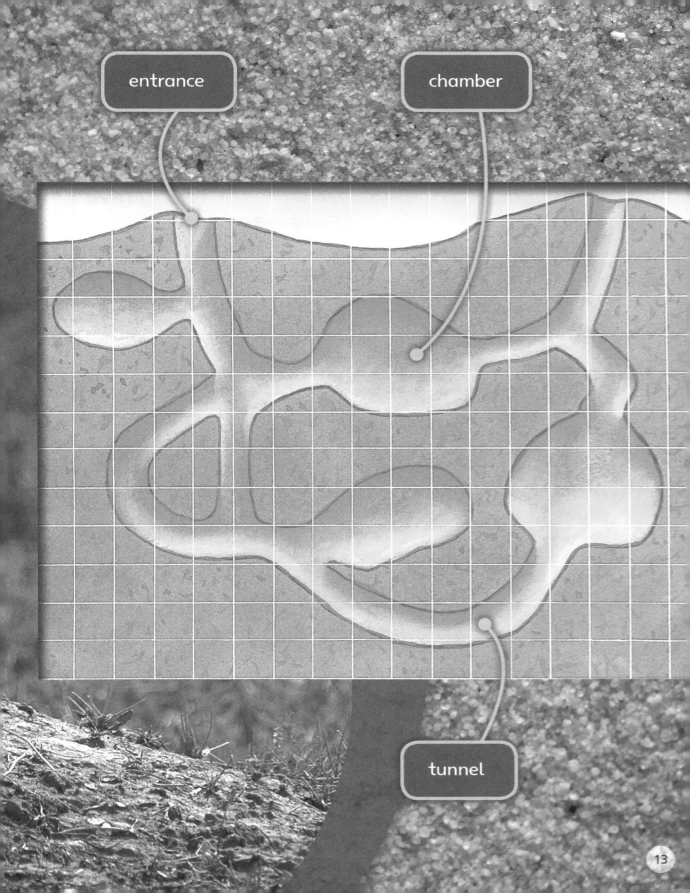

entrance

chamber

tunnel

Using plants and grasses

Some of the plants and grasses that grow on the plains are used by the prairie dogs for food. If they don't need a plant, they pull it out and leave it to die in the hot sun.

The plains provide a variety of food for the prairie dogs

A gyrfalcon searching the plains for prey

The dogs pull out the plants for two reasons. Predators need **ground cover** to hide them when they hunt, so without the plants, the dogs are safer from attack.

Also, when plants are pulled out, weeds grow more quickly. Their seeds and fruit give the prairie dogs some **variety** in the food they eat. Some plants, such as thistles, can hold a lot of water, and these give the dogs the **moisture** they need.

Prairie dog meetings

When prairie dogs meet, they need to know whether to be friendly or **hostile** to each other.

These meetings are important. Friendly meetings keep relationships good between members of each coterie. Hostile meetings show that **trespassers** are around and must be chased away.

Friend or enemy?

Kissing!

When two prairie dogs do not recognise each other, they meet in a particular way. They run towards each other. Then they turn their heads, open their mouths, bare their teeth, and 'kiss'. By doing this, they find out if they are friends or enemies.

If they decide they are friends, the dogs will often move off together and feed, keeping their bodies pressed against each other.

Friends!

Fighting

When two male dogs meet at the edge of their territories, they run towards each other and stop suddenly, face to face. They stare, flare their tails, chatter, and sniff each other. This is usually just **defensive** behaviour, but if they do start fighting, they bite, kick and charge at each other.

This sort of meeting can last up to five minutes, and may happen several times a day. Phew!

Enemies!

Grooming

Grooming each other is an important part of the dogs' daily social contact. It usually begins with the prairie dog 'kiss', and the two dogs then nibble and paw each other. Grooming helps to keep relationships friendly in each coterie.

Males and females, adults and young all groom each other. Pups love it, and will chase and crawl under adults to try to get their attention.

Being groomed is the *best* thing!

Barking and calling

The barks and calls that prairie dogs make have different meanings. The ordinary friendly bark is usually a short 'yip'. But when a dog senses that a predator is nearby, it gives a high-pitched call to warn other dogs. Each call is different and gives information about the type of predator.

A prairie dog giving
a warning call

Pups practise calls and barks, too.
Sometimes, they put so much energy into
their call that they lose their balance
and tumble backwards!

It's OK now!

Another type of call is the 'all-clear'. This call is a loud and clear signal that the predator has gone, and that everyone can feel safe again. The dog rises on its hind legs with its nose pointed straight up and its front feet pushed out in front of it. Sometimes, the call is so forceful that it lifts the dog off the ground!

Other dogs in the area will repeat the call, so the message is passed on throughout the coterie.

Is it safe to come out yet?

Giving the
all-clear call

A day in the life of a black-tailed prairie dog

A typical day consists of looking for food, keeping friendly with other dogs, cleaning burrows and watching out for predators.

Look-out duty

So much food!

Bringing fresh bedding to the burrow

What shall we do today?

The dogs spend most of the hot summer days sleeping in their burrows. They come out in the morning and evening. In cool or cloudy weather, they might come out shortly after sunrise and stay above ground all day. They only return to the burrow around sunset. In rainy weather, they stay in their burrows.

Quiz

1 Why are prairie dogs called 'dogs'?

   a Because they chew bones.
   b Because they like to go for walks.
   c Because they make a barking noise.

2 Where do black-tailed prairie dogs live?

   a North America
   b Australia
   c China

3 Why do prairie dogs build mounds?

   a So that the burrow entrance can't be seen.
   b To stop rain water coming into the burrows, and to use as a lookout.
   c To sit on and relax when it's sunny.

4 Which animal is the prairie dog related to?

   a meerkat
   b squirrel
   c guinea pig

5 What does a prairie dog do when it knows a predator is nearby?

   a It gives a warning call to other dogs.
   b It walks away slowly.
   c It pretends to be dead.

Answers on page 31

Glossary

bobcat   large North American wild cat

burrow   tunnel dug underground by a small animal

chamber   room

co-operatively   together

coyote   small North American wolf-like animal

defensive   trying not to be attacked

grooming   keeping neat and tidy

ground cover   small plants that grow thickly

herbivore   animal that eats mainly plants

hostile   acting like an enemy

litter   group of newborn animals

moisture   wetness

mound   small heap of something

prevent   keep from happening

rodent   animal that has large front teeth

social   living with others in an organised group

trespassers   someone who goes on to private land without permission

variety   number of different things

Index

barking   2, 24

bobcats   11

burrow   2, 4, 8, 10, 12, 28–29

calling   24, 26

chambers   4, 8–9, 11, 12–13

claws   2–3, 10

coteries   6, 8, 12, 16, 22

coyotes   11

defensive behaviour   20

entrance   4–5, 8, 10–11, 12–13

grasses   14

grooming   22

kissing   18, 22

litter   2

look-out   8, 10–11, 28

meetings   16

mound   10–11, 12

plains   4–5, 14

plants   14–15

predators   11, 15, 28

towns   4, 12

trespassers   16